T0028514

For Dana Meadows, who opened our eyes to the magic of TOGETHER. —L.S.

For Noah, Josh, and Ben. Together, my heart. —A.R.

A note for educators and caregivers:

Apart, Together playfully introduces cause and effect, prediction, and systems thinking, all building blocks of early childhood education. By highlighting scenes where two or more things create something altogether new and encouraging readers to look for interrelationships between objects, this book also introduces the concept of emergence, a scientific concept described by the adage *"The whole is greater than the sum of its parts."*

Balzer + Bray is an imprint of HarperCollins Publishers. • Apart, Together: A Book about Transformation • Text copyright © 2023 by Linda Booth Sweeney Illustrations copyright © 2023 by Ariel Rutland • All rights reserved. Manufactured in Italy. • No part of this book may be used or reproduced in any manner whatsoever without written permission except in the case of brief quotations embodied in critical articles and reviews. For information address HarperCollins Children's Books, a division of HarperCollins Publishers, 195 Broadway, New York, NY 10007 • www.harpercollinschildrens.com • ISBN 978-0-06-326461-8 • The artist used Procreate and Photoshop to create the illustrations for this book. • Typography by Dana Fritts • 23 24 25 26 27 RTLO 10 9 8 7 6 5 4 3 2 1 • First Edition

ETHER

a book about transformation

written by **Linda Booth Sweeney**   illustrated by **Ariel Rutland**

BALZER + BRAY
An Imprint of HarperCollinsPublishers

APART, blue is blue and yellow is yellow, but . . .

TOGETHER, they make green!

Seed and soil, sun and water

TOGETHER
make beans.

Bees and flowers

can make honey.

Flour, eggs, and sugar

can be yummy.

APART, bricks and blocks

are bricks
and blocks,

but . . . .

TOGETHER, they soar!

APART, players kick a ball, but . . .

TOGETHER, they score!

Soap and hands and water

can become foam.

Twigs and feathers

and
love

TOGETHER make a home.

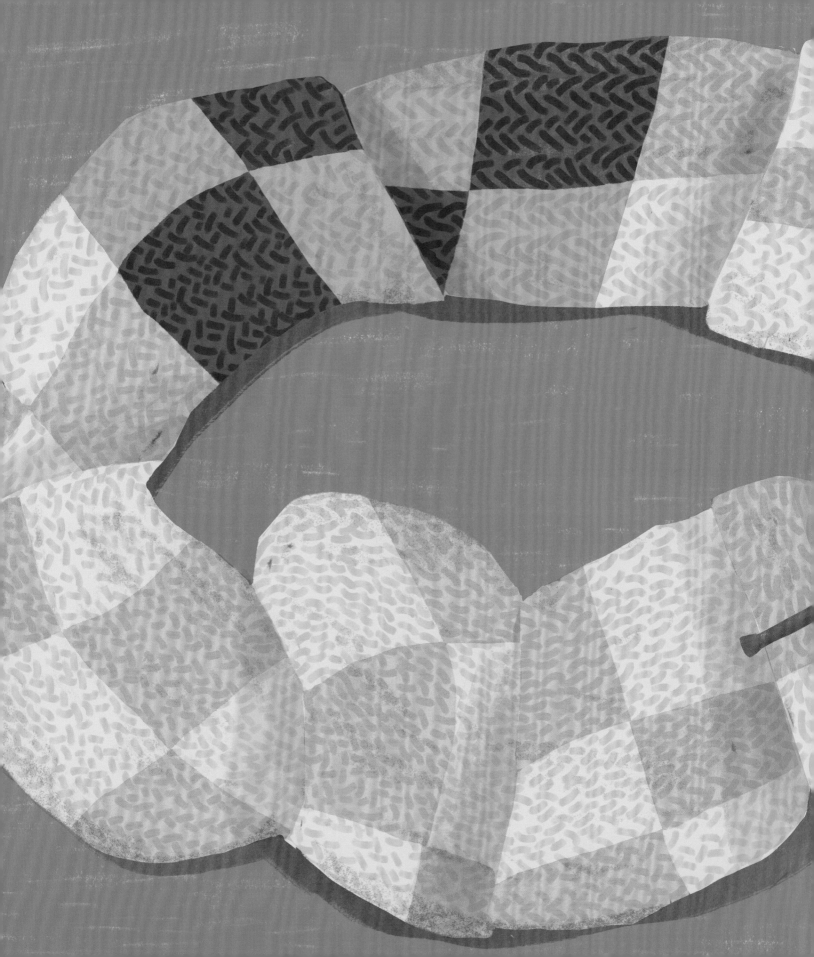